PIANO/VOCAL/GUITAR

THE BEST OF RODGERS & HAMMERSTEIN

ISBN 0-7935-2842-9

Performance rights to the Rodgers & Hammerstein musicals can be licensed from the R&H Theatre Library (Phone: 212/541-6900 Fax: 212/586-6155)

WILLIAMSON MUSIC
A RODGERS AND HAMMERSTEIN COMPANY

Exclusively Distributed by
Hal Leonard Publishing Corporation
7777 West Bluemound Road P.O. Box 13819 Milwaukee, WI 53213

Coyright © 1993 by WILLIAMSON MUSIC
International Copyright Secured   All Rights Reserved

BALI HA'I
from SOUTH PACIFIC

Lyrics by OSCAR HAMMERSTEIN II
Music by RICHARD RODGERS

REFRAIN (Slowly)

Ba - li Ha'i may call you an - y night, An - y

day. In your heart you'll hear it call you: "Come a -

way, Come a - way." Ba - li Ha'i will whis - per On the

wind of the sea: "Here am I, Your spe - cial

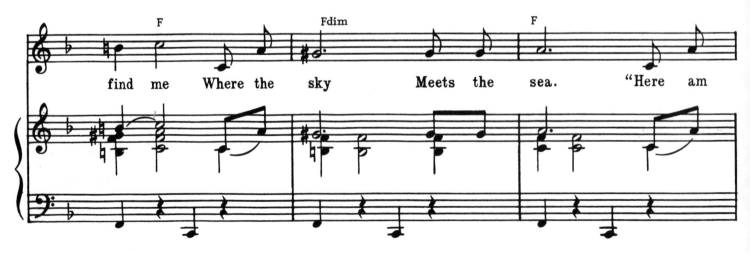

I, —— Your spe - cial is - land! Come to me, Come to

me!" Ba - li Ha'i, Ba - li Ha'i, Ba - li

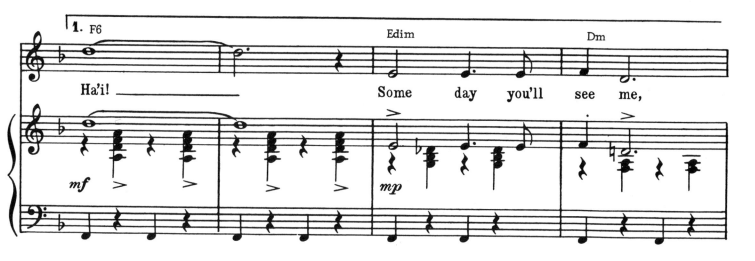

Ha'i! ——————— Some day you'll see me,

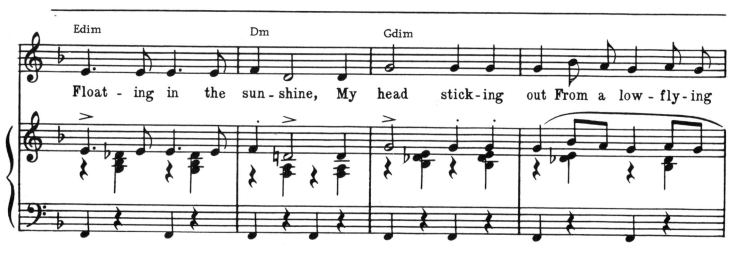

Float - ing in the sun - shine, My head stick - ing out From a low - fly - ing

cloud._____ You'll hear me call you,

Sing - ing through the sun - shine, Sweet and clear as can

be,_____ "Come to me, Here am I, come to

me!"_____ Ba - li Ha'i! _____

CLIMB EV'RY MOUNTAIN
from THE SOUND OF MUSIC

Lyrics by OSCAR HAMMERSTEIN II
Music by RICHARD RODGERS

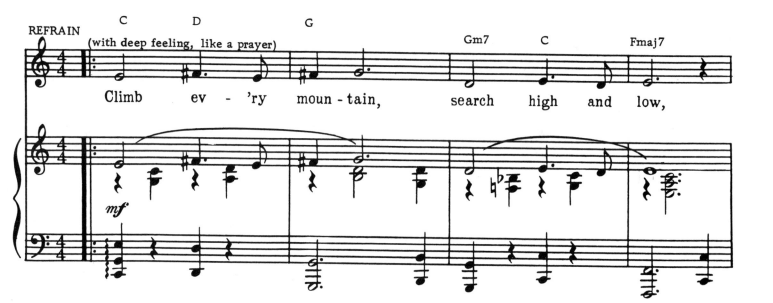

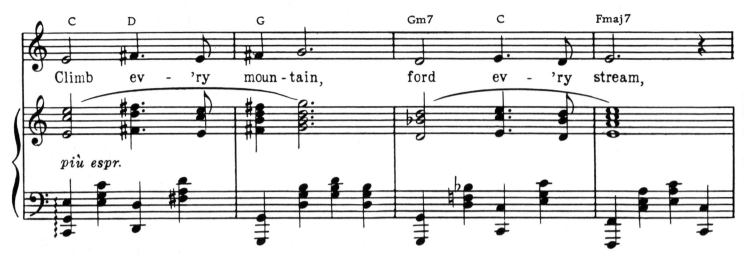

Climb ev - 'ry moun - tain, ford ev - 'ry stream,

Fol - low ev - 'ry rain - bow, till you find your dream! A

dream that will need all the love you can give,_____

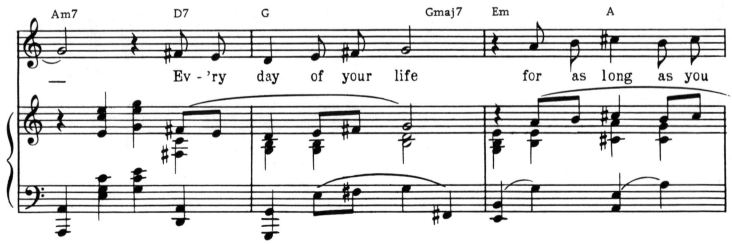

___ Ev - 'ry day of your life for as long as you

live. _____ Climb ev - 'ry moun - tain,

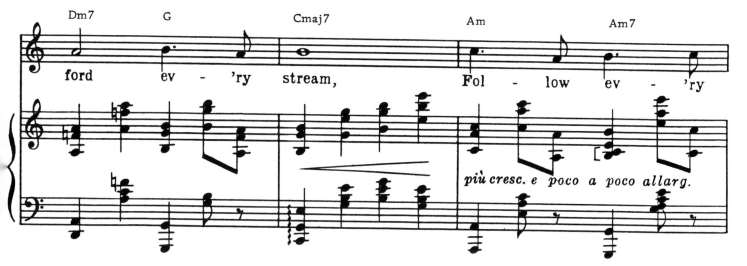

ford ev - 'ry stream, Fol - low ev - 'ry

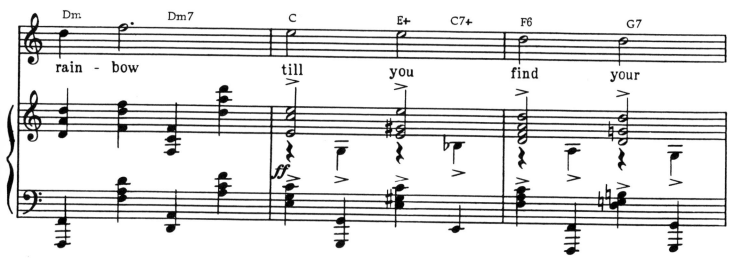

rain - bow till you find your

1. dream!

2. dream! _____

DO I LOVE YOU BECAUSE YOU'RE BEAUTIFUL?

from CINDERELLA

Lyrics by OSCAR HAMMERSTEIN II
Music by RICHARD RODGERS

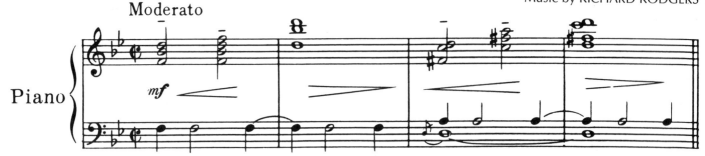

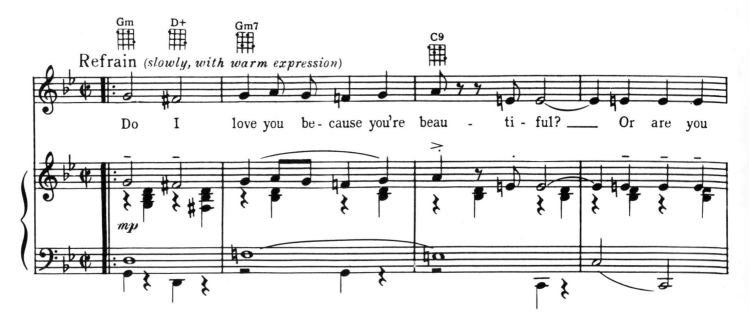

Do I love you be-cause you're beau - ti-ful? ___ Or are you

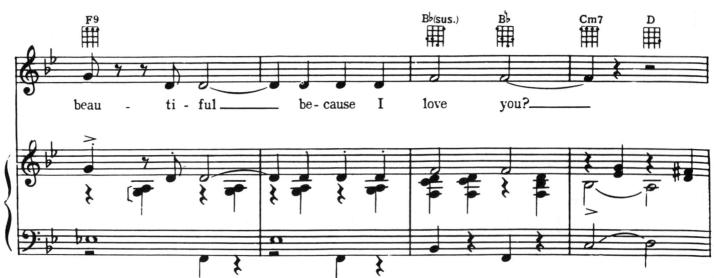

beau - ti-ful ___ be - cause I love you? ___

Am I mak-ing be-lieve I see in you ____ A girl too

love - ly to ____ be real - ly true?

Do I want you be - cause you're

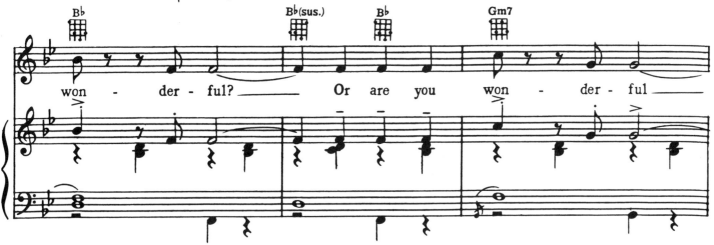

won - der - ful? ____ Or are you won - der - ful ____

Be - cause I want you? _____

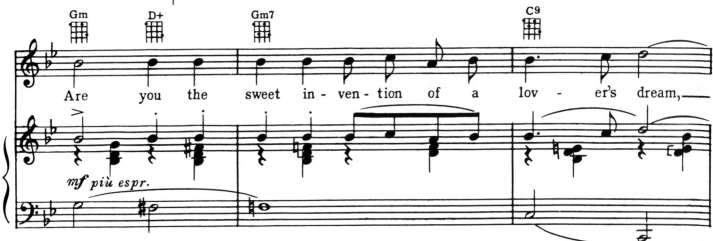

Are you the sweet in - ven - tion of a lov - er's dream, _____

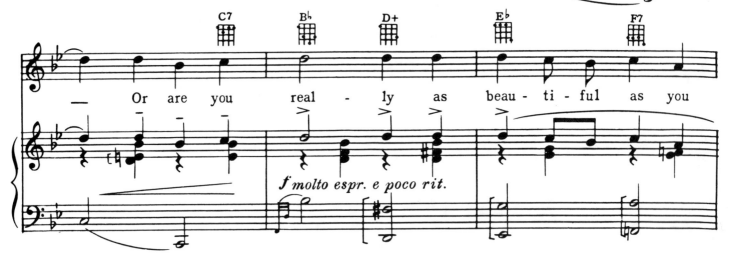

Or are you real - ly as beau - ti - ful as you

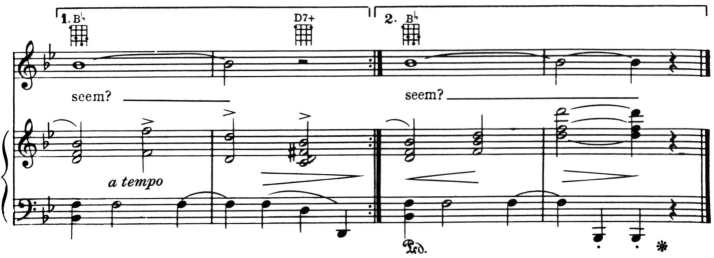

seem? _____   seem? _____

I'M GONNA WASH THAT MAN RIGHT OUTA MY HAIR

from SOUTH PACIFIC

Lyrics by OSCAR HAMMERSTEIN II
Music by RICHARD RODGERS

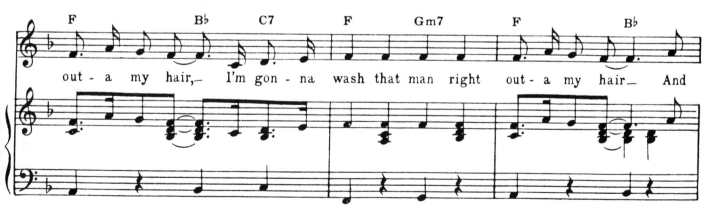

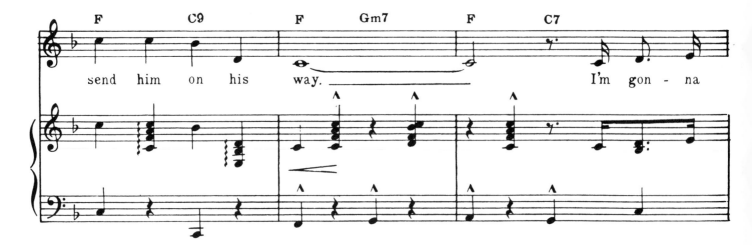

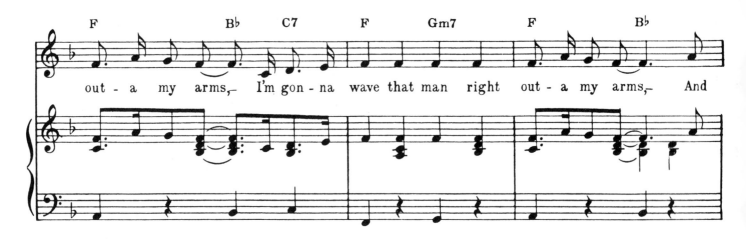

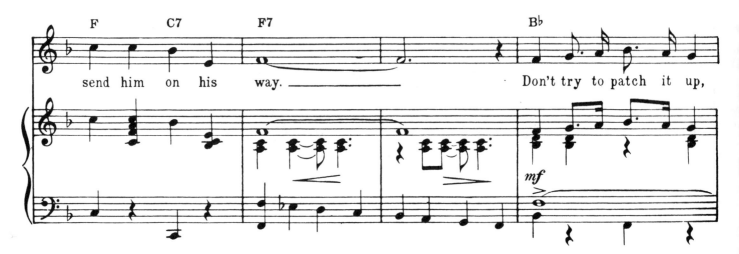

Tear it up, tear it up! Wash him out, dry him out, Push him out, fly him out,

Can-cel him and let him go! Yea, sis-ter!__ I'm gon-na

wash that man right out-a my hair,__ I'm gon-na wash that man right

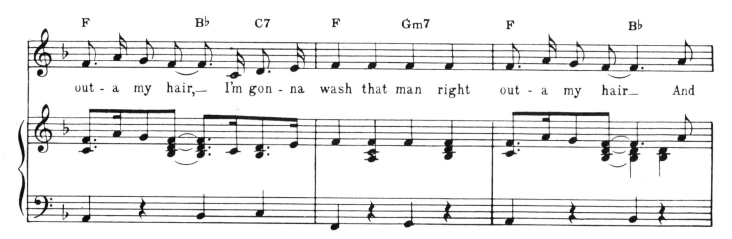

out-a my hair,__ I'm gon-na wash that man right out-a my hair__ And

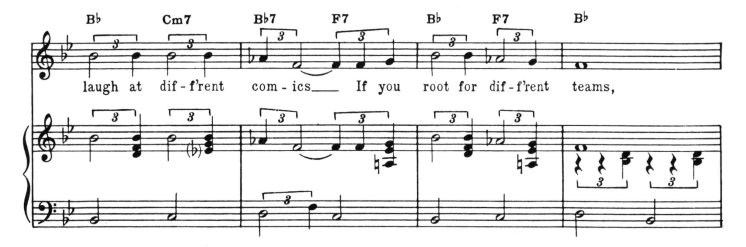

laugh at dif-f'rent com-ics___ If you root for dif-f'rent teams,

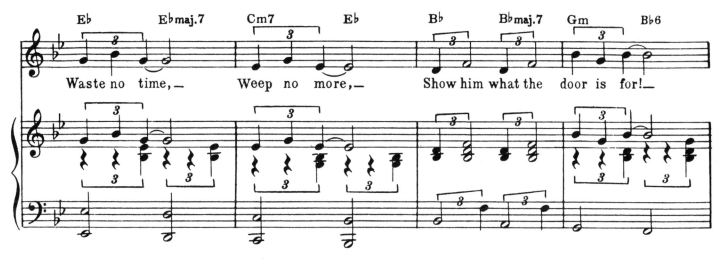

Waste no time,— Weep no more,— Show him what the door is for!___

Rub him out-a the roll-call___ And drum him out-a your dreams. Oh,

no!————————————— Oh, no!—————— I'm gon-na

EDELWEISS
from THE SOUND OF MUSIC

Lyrics by OSCAR HAMMERSTEIN
Music by RICHARD RODGER

Slowly

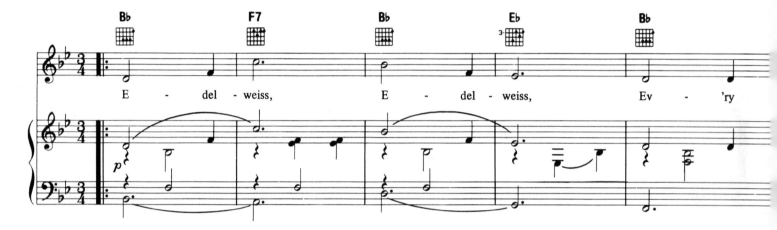

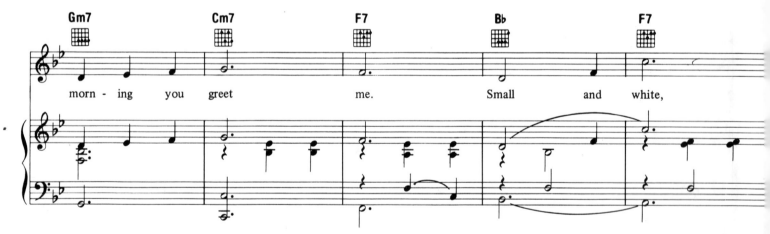

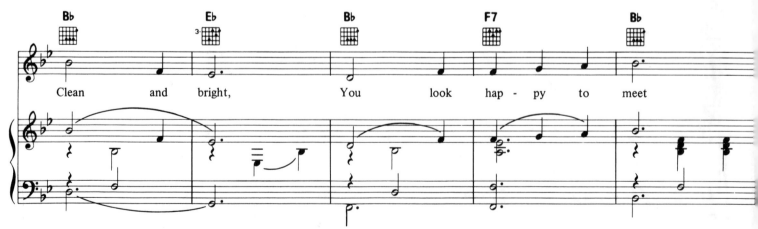

GETTING TO KNOW YOU

from THE KING AND I

Lyrics by OSCAR HAMMERSTEIN II
Music by RICHARD RODGERS

It's a ver-y an-cient say - ing But a true and hon-est

thought, That if you be-come a teach - er, by your

pu-pils you'll be taught. As a teach - er, I've been

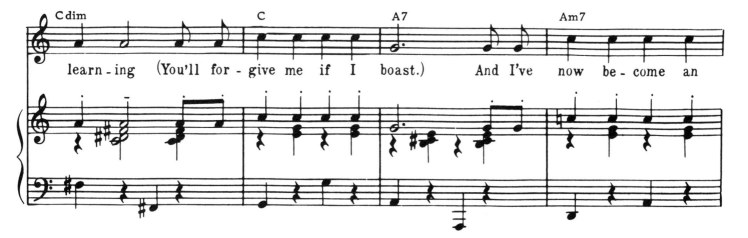

learn-ing (You'll for-give me if I boast.) And I've now be-come an

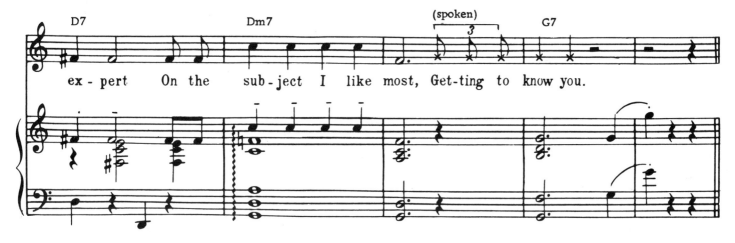

ex-pert On the sub-ject I like most, Get-ting to know you.

REFRAIN (gracefully, not fast)

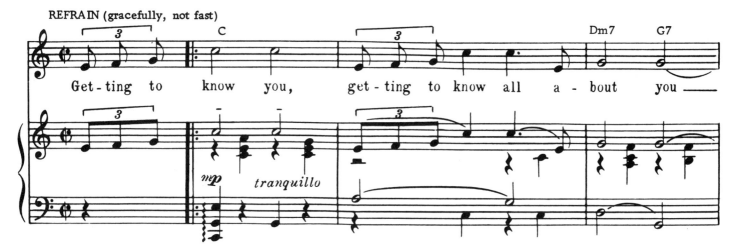

Get-ting to know you, get-ting to know all a-bout you

Get-ting to like you, get-ting to hope you like me

Get-ting to know you, Put-ting it my way, but nice-ly ___

You are pre-cise - ly My cup of tea! ___

Get-ting to know you, get-ting to feel free and eas - y ___

When I am with you, get-ting to know what to say. ___

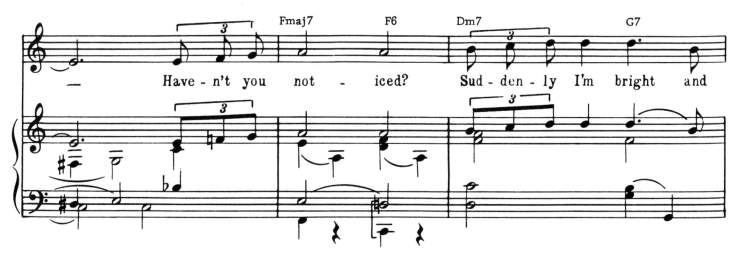

Have-n't you not - iced? Sud - den - ly I'm bright and

breez - y _____ Be - cause of all the beau - ti - ful and new

poco a poco cresc.

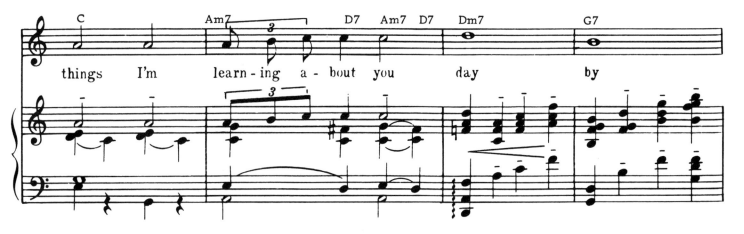

things I'm learn - ing a - bout you day by

day. _____ Get - ting to day. _____

HELLO, YOUNG LOVERS
from THE KING AND I

Lyrics by OSCAR HAMMERSTEIN II
Music by RICHARD RODGERS

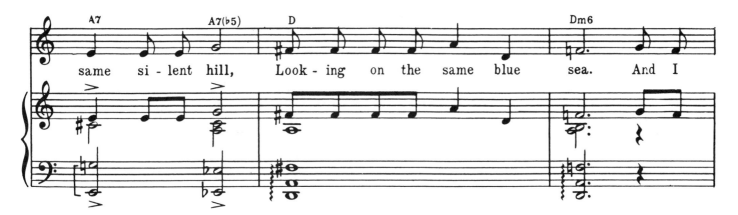

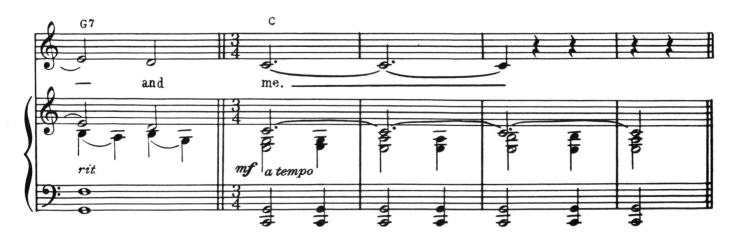

Refrain (Very moderately)

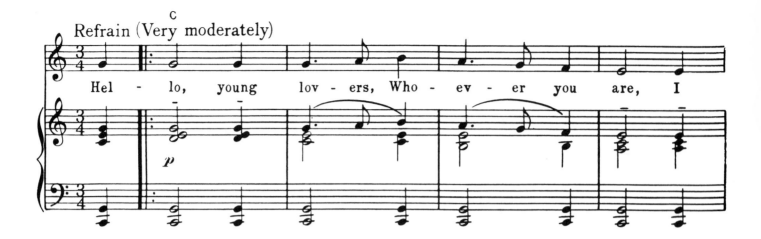

Hel - lo, young lov - ers, Who - ev - er you are, I

hope your trou - bles are few _____ All my good

wish - es go with you to - night ____ I've been in love like

you _____ Be brave, young lov - ers, and fol - low your

star, Be brave and faith - ful and true _____

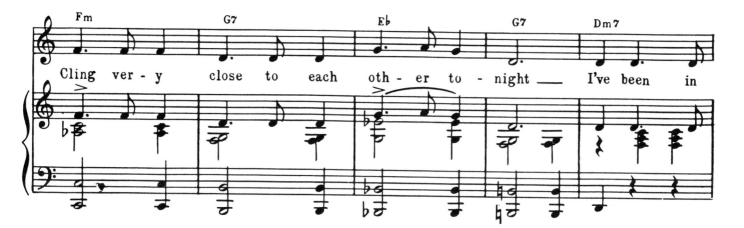

Cling ver - y close to each oth - er to - night ___ I've been in

love like you. _____ I know how it feels to have

wings on your heels, And to fly down a street in a trance. ___

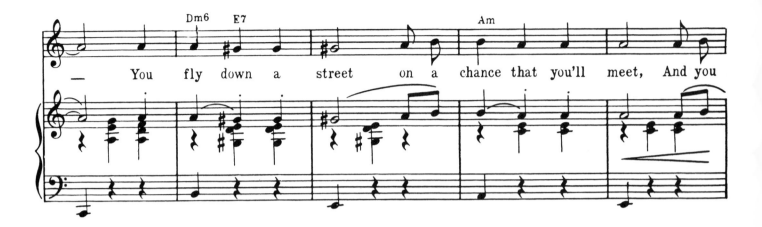

hap - py to - night _____ I've had a love of my

own, _____ I've had a love of my

own like yours, I've had a love of my

own.   Hel -   own. _____

I HAVE DREAMED

from THE KING AND I

Lyrics by OSCAR HAMMERSTEIN II
Music by RICHARD RODGERS

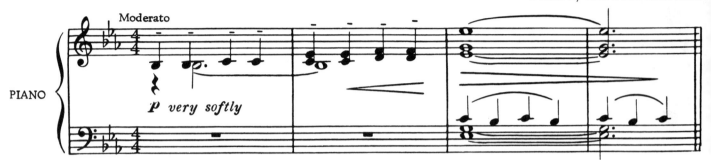

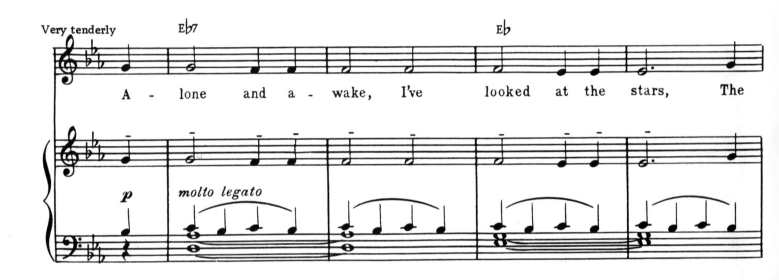

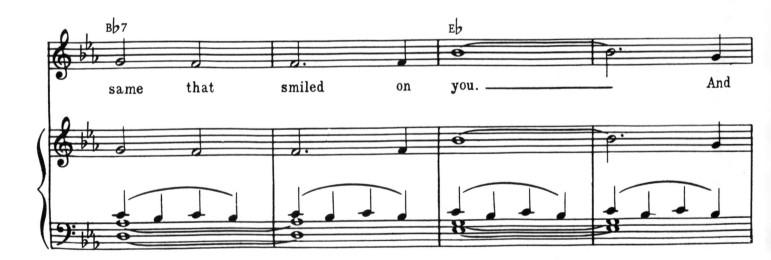

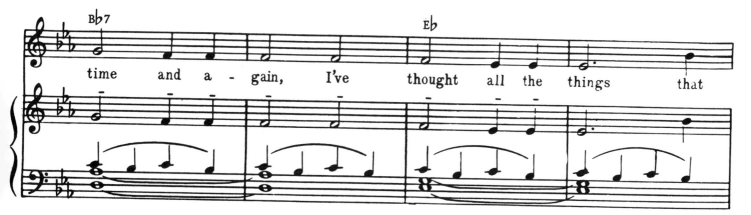

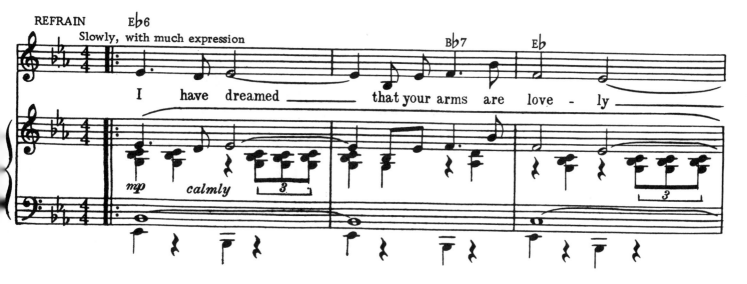

I have dreamed ___ ev-'ry word you'll whis - per ___

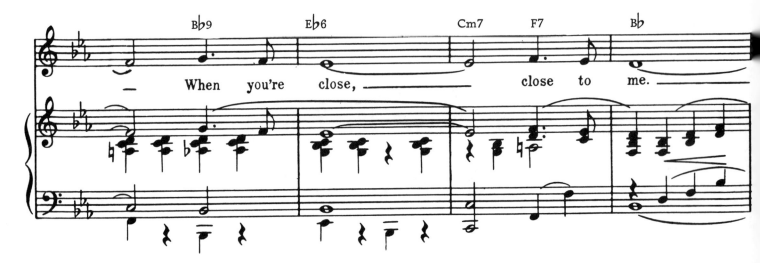

When you're close, ___ close to me. ___

How you look ___ in the glow of eve - ning ___

I have dreamed ___ and en - joyed the

view _____ In these dreams I've loved you so that by

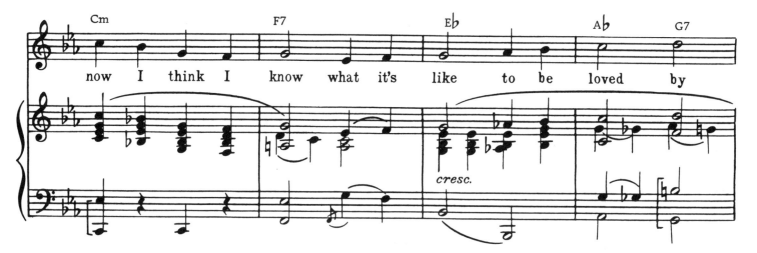

now I think I know what it's like to be loved by

you _____ I will love be - ing loved by

you. _____ you. _____

I WHISTLE A HAPPY TUNE

from THE KING AND I

Lyrics by OSCAR HAMMERSTEIN II
Music by RICHARD RODGERS

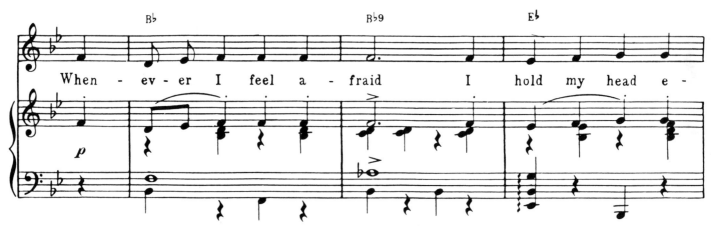

shoes I strike a care-less pose And whis-tle a hap-py

tune And no-one ev-er knows I'm a-fraid _____

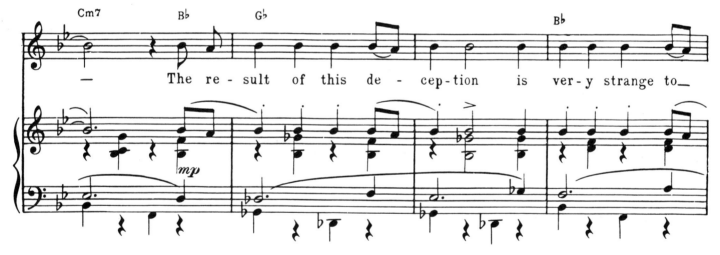

— The re-sult of this de-cep-tion is ver-y strange to_

tell For when I fool the peo-ple I fear, I

fool my-self as well! I whis-tle a hap-py tune And

ev-'ry sin-gle time The hap-pi-ness in the tune con-

vin-ces me that I'm not a-fraid.

Coda

Make be-lieve you're brave And the trick will take you far.

IF I LOVED YOU
from CAROUSEL

Lyrics by OSCAR HAMMERSTEIN II
Music by RICHARD RODGERS

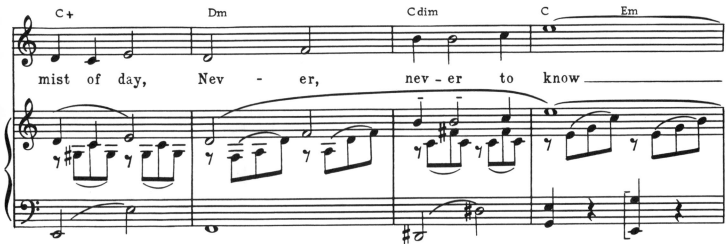

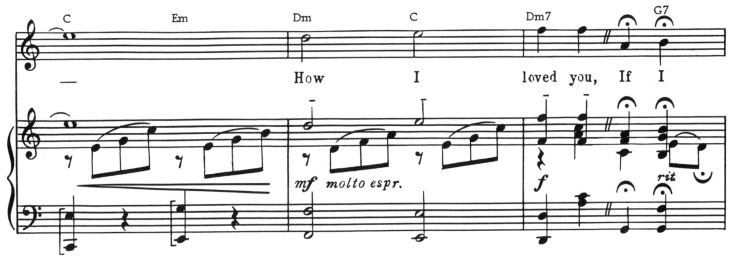

IT MIGHT AS WELL BE SPRING

from STATE FAIR

Lyrics by OSCAR HAMMERSTEIN II
Music by RICHARD RODGERS

The things I used to like I don't like an-y more, I want a lot of oth-er things I've nev-er had be-fore. It's just like moth-er says, I "sit a-round and mope" Pre-tend-ing I am won-der-ful and know-ing I'm a dope.

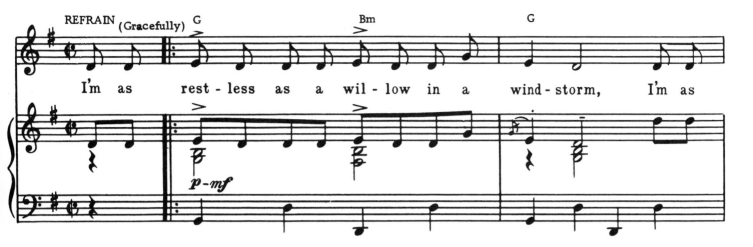

REFRAIN (Gracefully)

I'm as rest-less as a wil-low in a wind-storm, I'm as

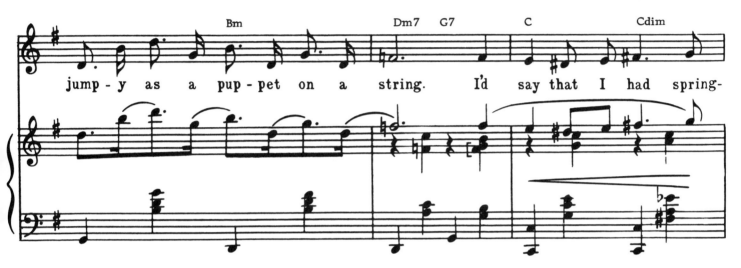

jump-y as a pup-pet on a string. I'd say that I had spring-

fe - ver, But I know it is - n't spring. I am

star-ry eyed and vague-ly dis-con - tent - ed, Like a night-in-gale with-out a song to

gid-dy as a ba-by on a swing. I have-n't seen a cro-cus or a

rose - bud, or a rob-in on the wing, But I feel so gay in a

mel-an-cho-ly way that it might as well be spring. It might as well be

spring!   I'm as   spring! _____

JUNE IS BUSTIN' OUT ALL OVER
from CAROUSEL

Lyrics by OSCAR HAMMERSTEIN II
Music by RICHARD RODGERS

LOVE, LOOK AWAY
from FLOWER DRUM SONG

Lyrics by OSCAR HAMMERSTEIN II
Music by RICHARD RODGERS

They say you "make the world go 'round," They say you "con - quer all."

Love, won't you please stop con-q'ring me? Take some-one your size, I'm small;_ Too

small to fight a - gainst the odds, Too tired to chase ro - mance,

Know-ing I need one man a-lone, And know-ing I have no chance.____

REFRAIN

Moderato espressivo

Love, look a - way!____ Love, look a - way from

me. Fly, when you pass my door, Fly and get lost at

sea. Call it a day.____ Love, let us say we're

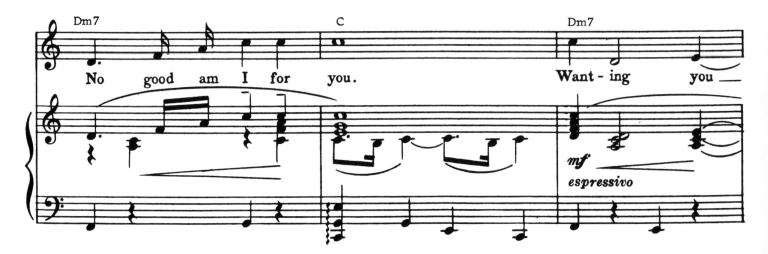

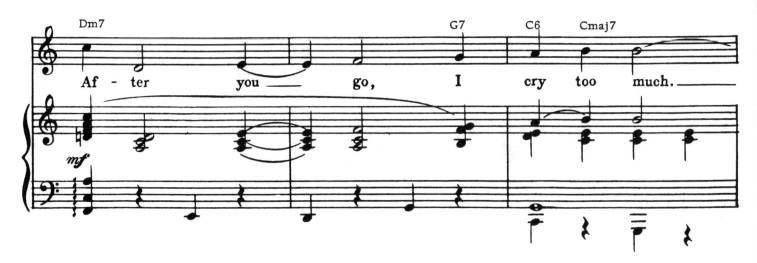

Love, look a - way.___

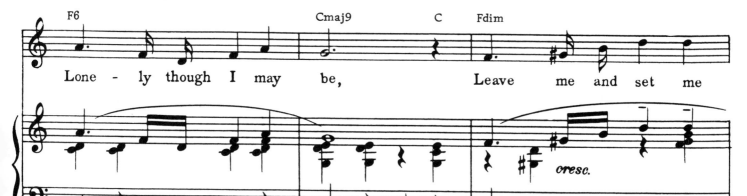

Lone - ly though I may be, Leave me and set me

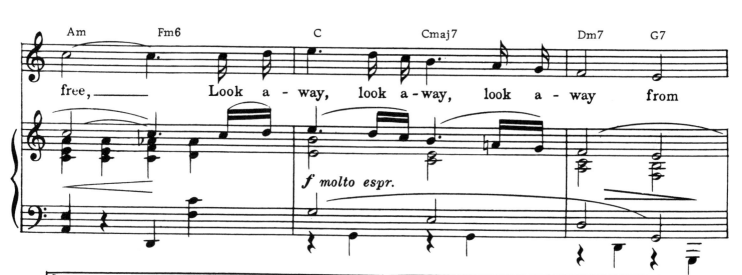

free,___ Look a - way, look a - way, look a - way from

me. me.___

MY FAVORITE THINGS
from THE SOUND OF MUSIC

Lyrics by OSCAR HAMMERSTEIN II
Music by RICHARD RODGERS

Girls in white dress-es with blue sat-in sash-es, Snow-flakes that
stay on my nose and eye-lash-es, Sil-ver white win-ters that
melt in-to springs, These are a few of my fa-vor-ite things.

When the dog bites, When the bee stings,

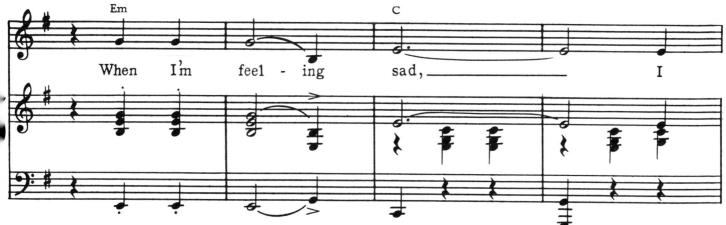

When I'm feel-ing sad,_____ I

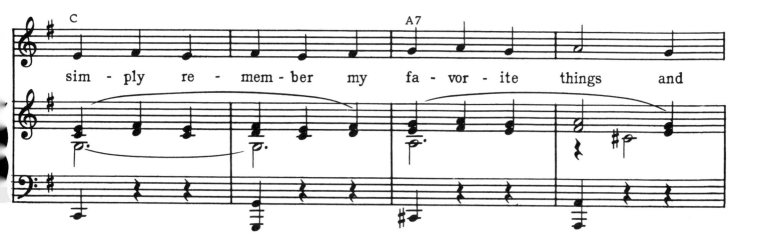

sim-ply re-mem-ber my fa-vor-ite things and

then I don't feel so bad._____

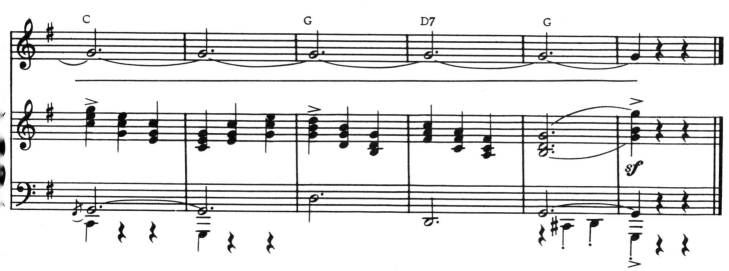

NO OTHER LOVE

from ME AND JULIET

Lyrics by OSCAR HAMMERSTEIN II
Music by RICHARD RODGERS

PIANO

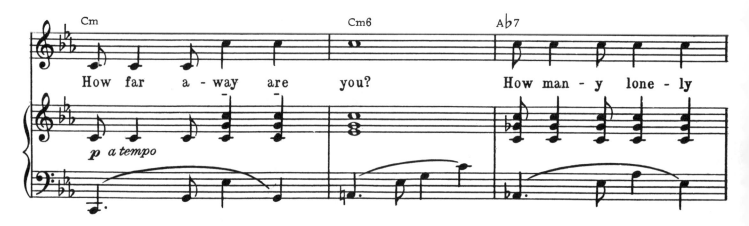

How far a-way are you? How man-y lone-ly

sighs, dear? How man-y weep-ing skies, dear?

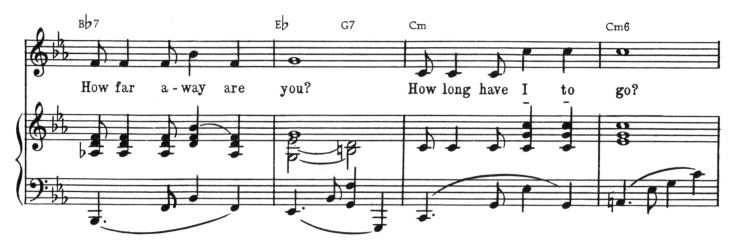

How far a-way are you? How long have I to go?

How man - y moons to see, dear, Till you come back to me, dear?

When will I know? When will I know?

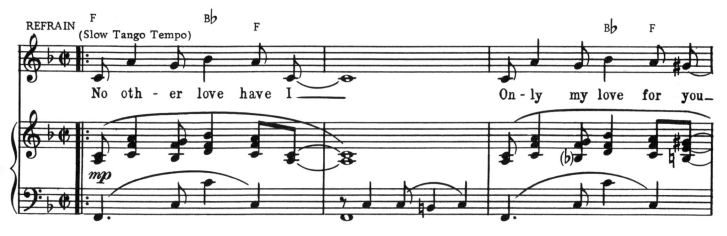

REFRAIN (Slow Tango Tempo)

No oth - er love have I ___ On - ly my love for you ___

___ On - ly the dream we knew ___

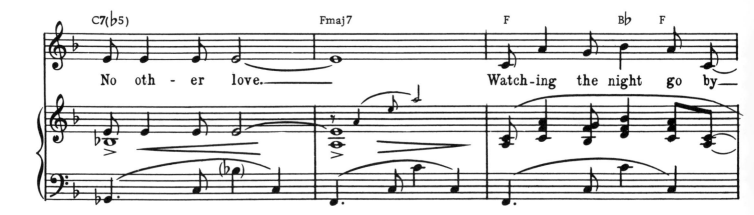

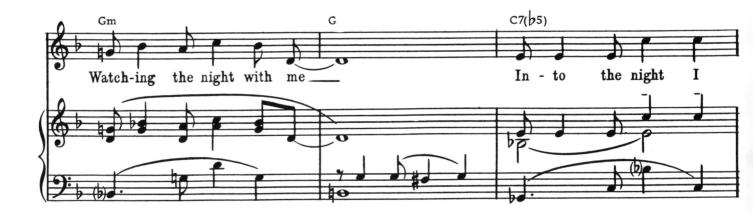

free, free from doubt and free _____

_____ from long-ing. In-to your arms I'll fly__ Locked in your arms I'll stay__

_____ Wait-ing to hear you say__ No oth - er love have

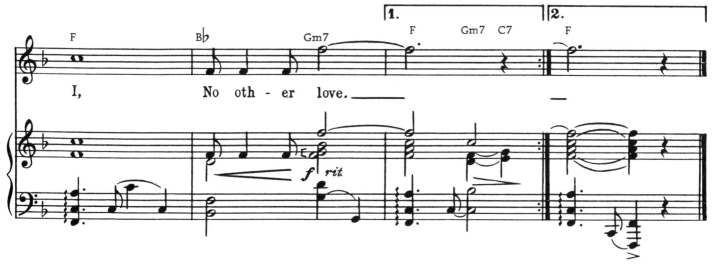

I, No oth - er love. _____ —

OKLAHOMA
from OKLAHOMA!

Lyrics by OSCAR HAMMERSTEIN II
Music by RICHARD RODGERS

* *Names of chords for Ukulele and Banjo.*
Symbols for Guitar.

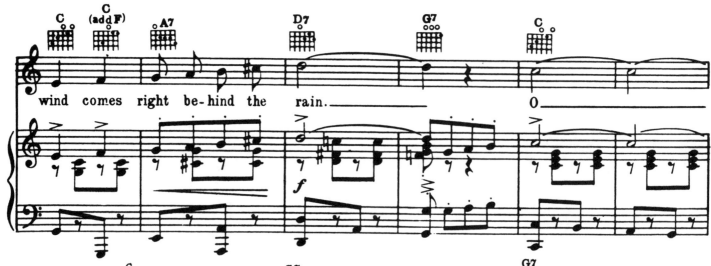

wind comes right be-hind the rain._____ O_____

-k - la-hom-a, Ev-'ry night my hon-ey lamb and I_____ sit a-

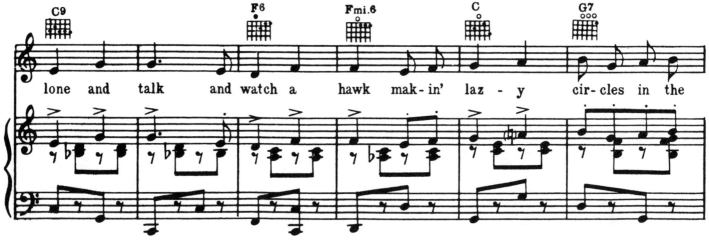

lone and talk and watch a hawk mak-in' laz - y cir-cles in the

sky._____ We know we be - long to the land_____

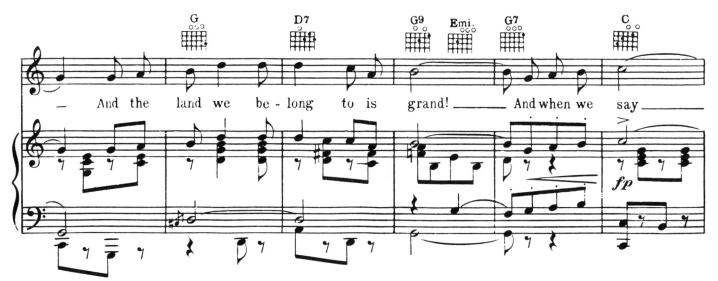

And the land we be-long to is grand! ____ And when we say ____

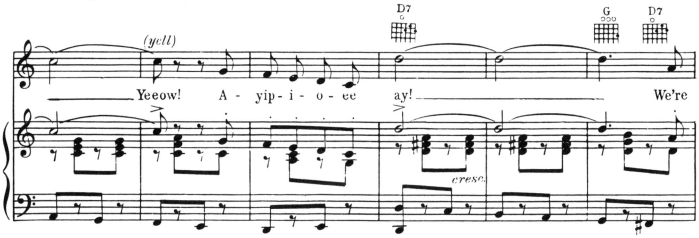

____ Yeeow! A - yip-i - o - ee ay! ____ We're

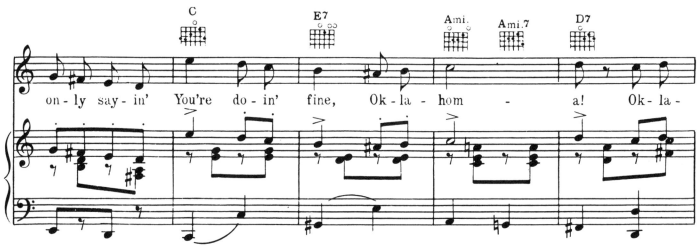

on-ly say-in' You're do-in' fine, Ok-la-hom - a! Ok-la-

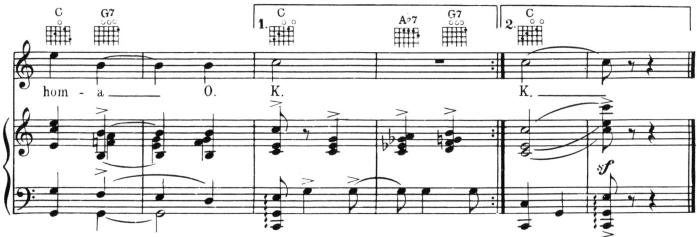

hom - a ____ O. K.   K. ____

OH, WHAT A BEAUTIFUL MORNIN'
from OKLAHOMA!

Lyrics by OSCAR HAMMERSTEIN II
Music by RICHARD RODGERS

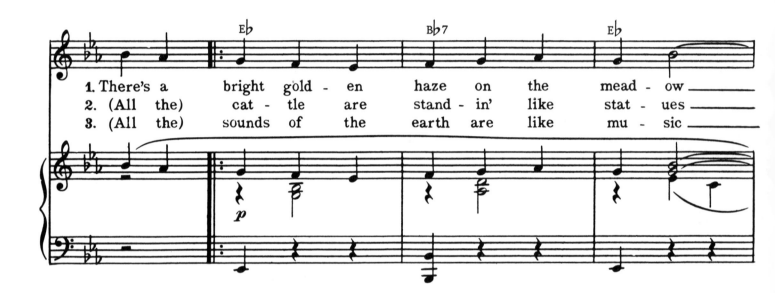

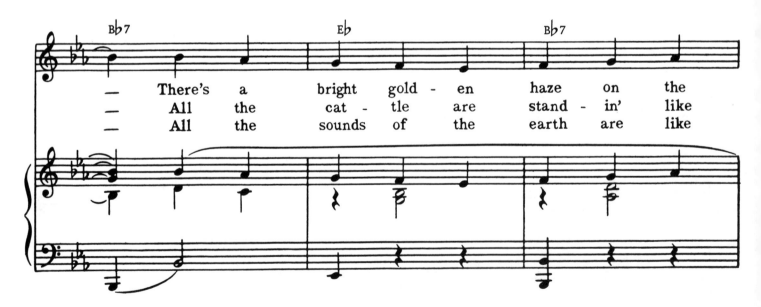

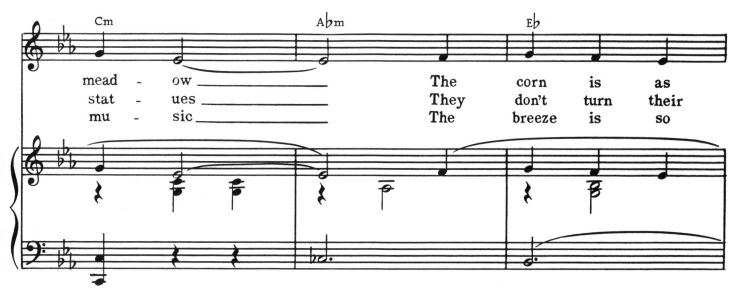

meadow _____ The corn is as
statues _____ They don't turn their
music _____ The breeze is so

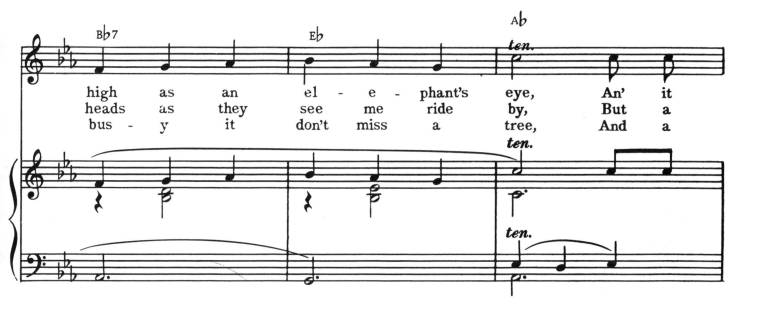

high as an el - e - phant's eye, An' it
heads as they see me ride by, But a
bus - y it don't miss a tree, And a

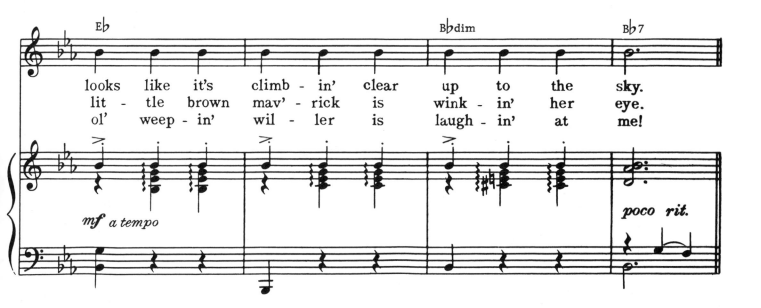

looks like it's climb - in' clear up to the sky.
lit - tle brown mav' - rick is wink - in' her eye.
ol' weep - in' wil - ler is laugh - in' at me!

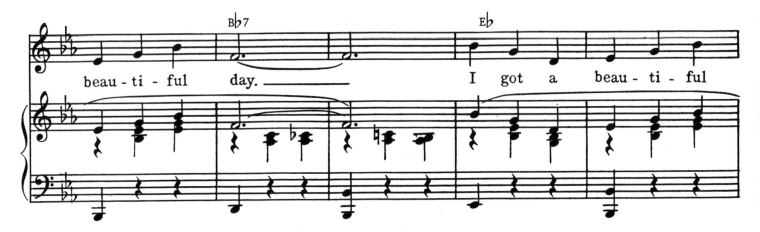

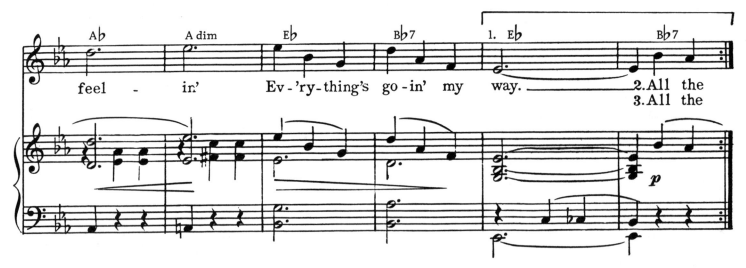

SOME ENCHANTED EVENING

from SOUTH PACIFIC

Lyrics by OSCAR HAMMERSTEIN II
Music by RICHARD RODGERS

Some en-chant-ed eve - ning ___ You may see a stran - ger, ___

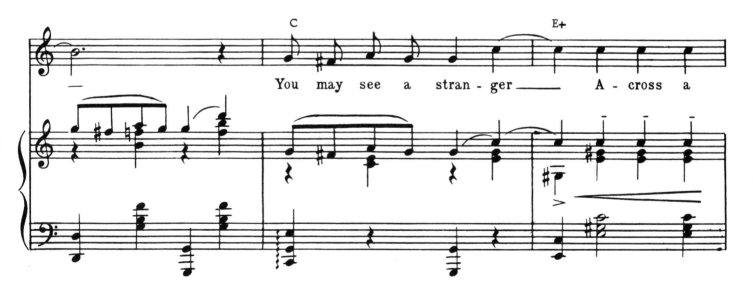

You may see a stran - ger ___ A - cross a

crowd - ed room   And some-how you   know,_____ You know e - ven

then _____ That some-where you'll   see her a - gain and a -

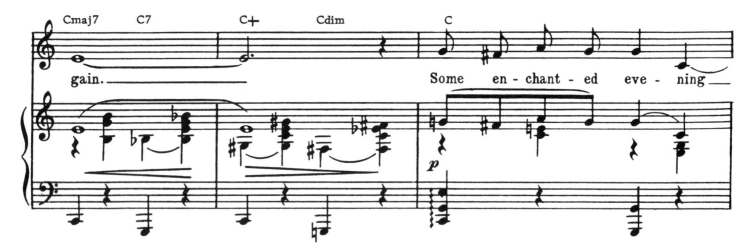

gain._____   Some en - chant - ed eve - ning ___

Some - one may   be laugh - ing,___

74

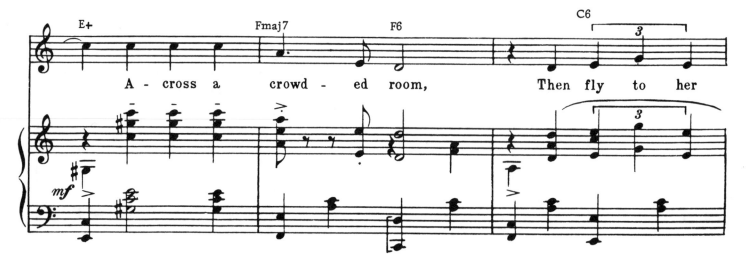

side _____ And make her your own, _____ Or all through your

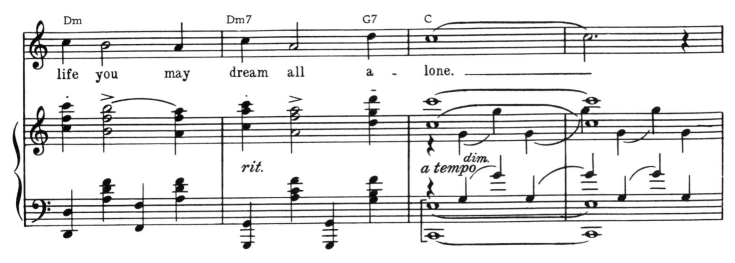

life you may dream all a - lone. _____

Once you have found her, Nev - er let her go. Once you have found her,

Nev - er let her go! _____

PEOPLE WILL SAY WE'RE IN LOVE

from OKLAHOMA!

Lyrics by OSCAR HAMMERSTEIN II
Music by RICHARD RODGERS

I know a way to prove what they say is quite un-true.___
Grant-in' your wish, I carved our i-ni-tials on the tree!

Here is the gist, a prac-ti-cal list of "don'ts" for you.___
Jist keep a slice of all the ad-vice you give so free.___

REFRAIN

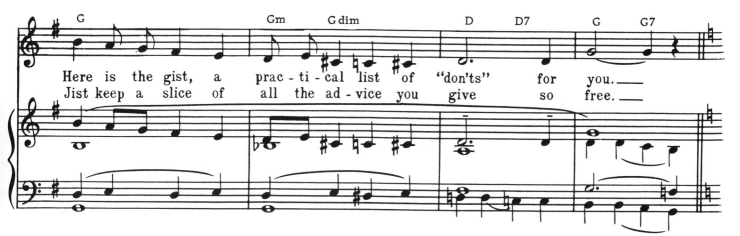

Don't throw___ bou-quets at me___ Don't please___
Don't praise___ my charm too much___ Don't look___

— my folks too much___ Don't laugh___ at my
— so vane with me___ Don't stand___ in the

THE SURREY WITH THE FRINGE ON TOP

from OKLAHOMA!

Lyrics by OSCAR HAMMERSTEIN
Music by RICHARD RODGERS

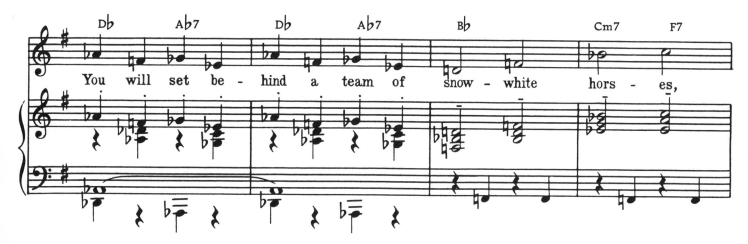

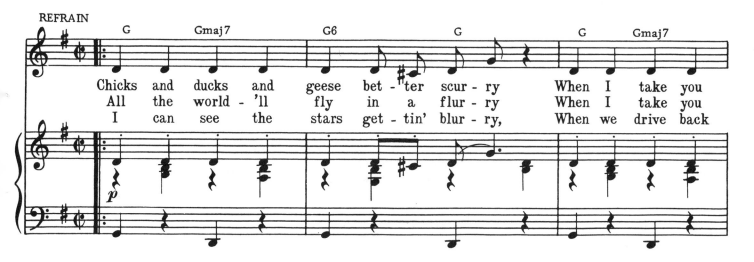

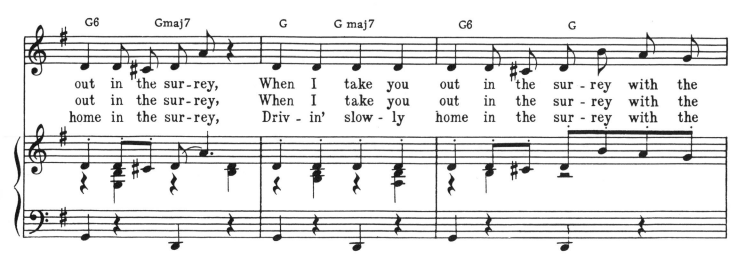

THE SOUND OF MUSIC
from THE SOUND OF MUSIC

Lyrics by OSCAR HAMMERSTEIN II
Music by RICHARD RODGERS

My day in the hills has come to an end, I

know. A star has come out to tell me it's time to go. But

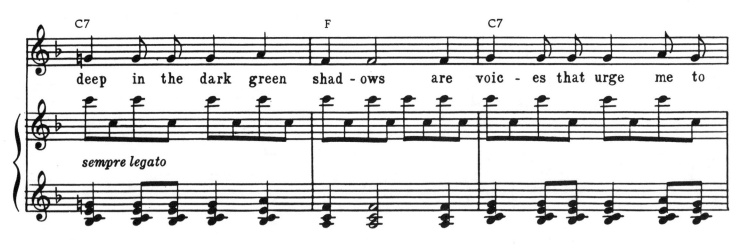

deep in the dark green shad-ows are voic-es that urge me to

stay. So I pause and I wait and I lis-ten for one more sound, For

one more love-ly thing that the hills might say.

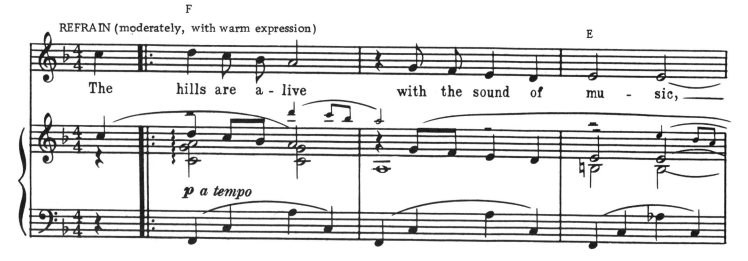

REFRAIN (moderately, with warm expression)

The hills are a-live with the sound of mu - sic,

With songs they have sung for a thou - sand

years. The hills fill my heart with the sound of

mu - sic. _____ My heart wants to sing ev -'ry song it

hears. _____ My heart wants to beat like the wings of the

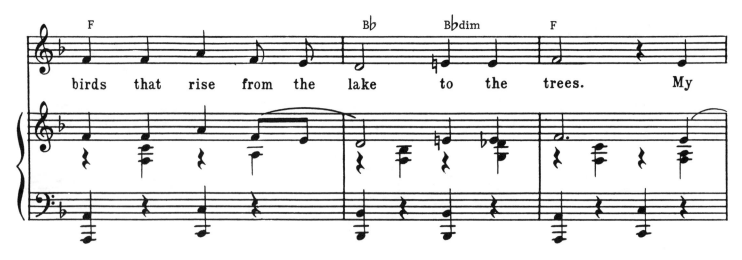

birds that rise from the lake to the trees. My

heart wants to sigh like a chime that flies from a church on a

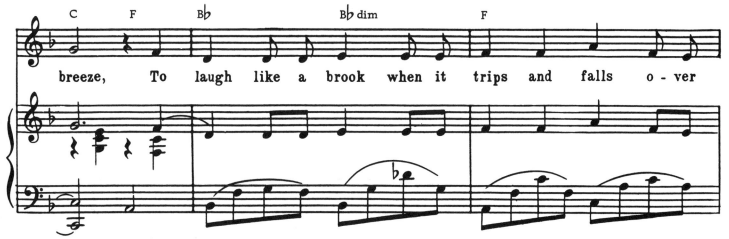

breeze, To laugh like a brook when it trips and falls o - ver

stones on its way, To sing through the night like a

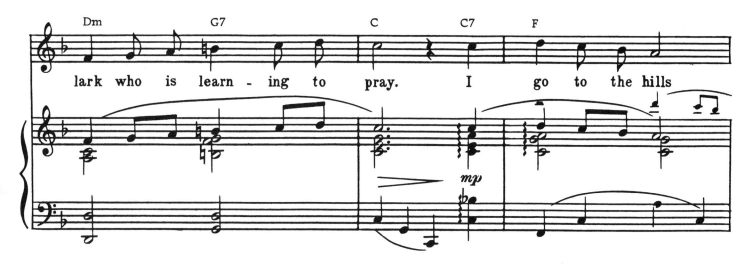

lark who is learn - ing to pray. I go to the hills

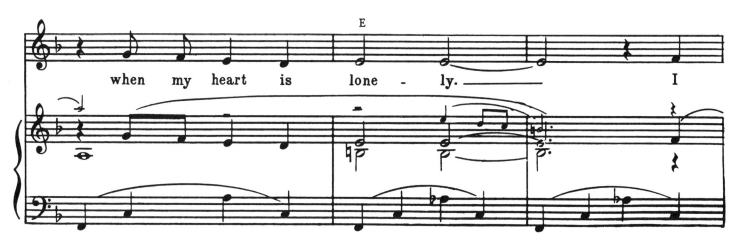

when my heart is lone - ly. _____ I

88

know I will hear   what I've heard be - fore.____

____ My heart will be blessed   with the sound of

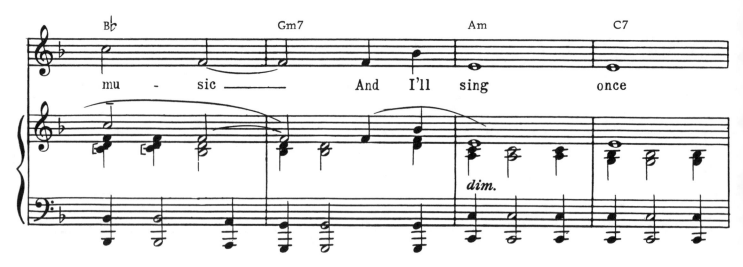

mu - sic ____   And I'll sing   once

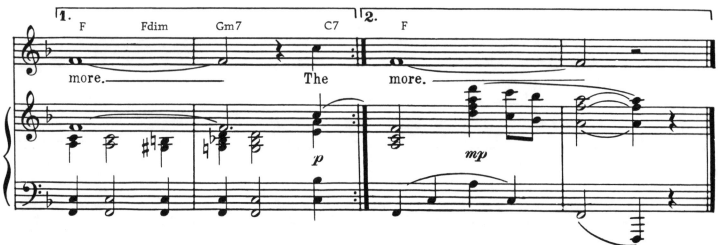

more.____   The more.____

THERE IS NOTHIN' LIKE A DAME

from SOUTH PACIFIC

Lyrics by OSCAR HAMMERSTEIN II
Music by RICHARD RODGERS

We got sun-light on the sand, We got moon-light on the sea, We got man-goes and ba-

na-nas You can pick right off a tree, We got vol-ley ball and ping pong And a lot of dan-dy

games! What ain't we got? We ain't got dames! _____ We get

There is noth-in' like a dame, _____ Noth-in' in the

world, _____ There is noth-in' you can name That is

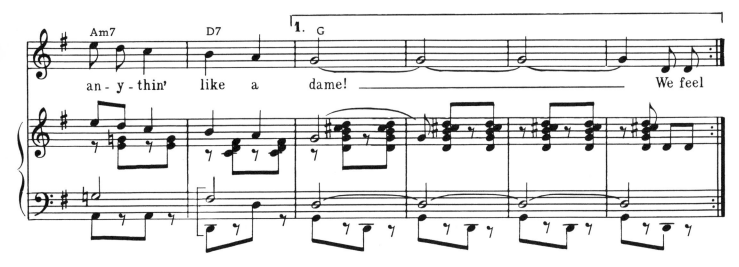

an-y-thin' like a dame! _____ We feel

dame! _____ There are no

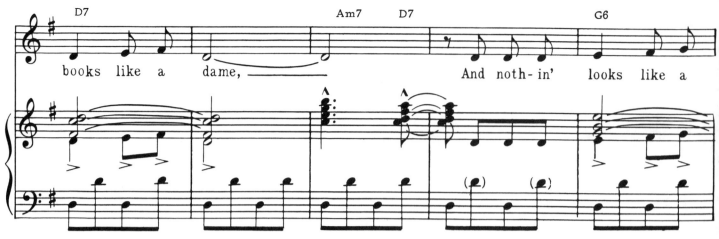

books like a dame, _____ And noth-in' looks like a

dame. _____ There are no drinks like a dame, _____

poco a poco crescendo

And noth-in' thinks like a dame, _____

And noth-in' acts like a dame, _____ Or at-

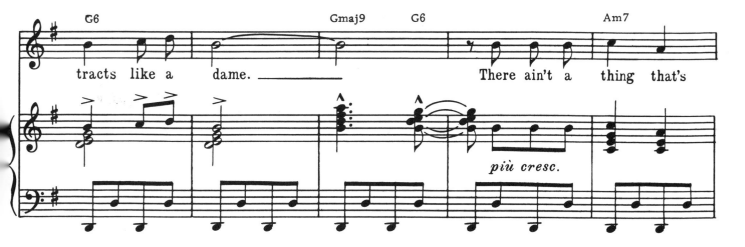

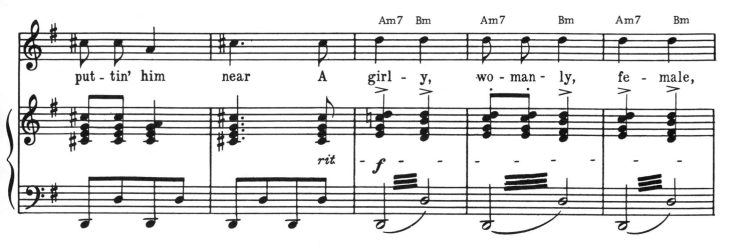

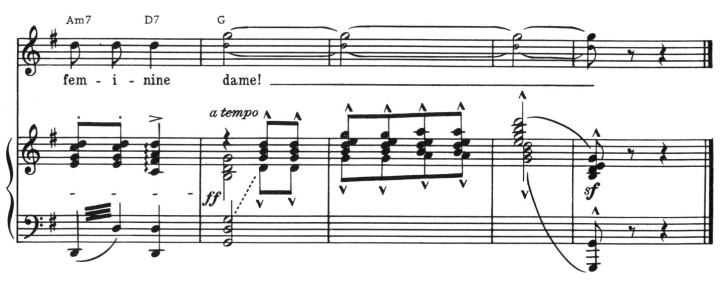

THIS NEARLY WAS MINE

from SOUTH PACIFIC

Lyrics by OSCAR HAMMERSTEIN II
Music by RICHARD RODGERS

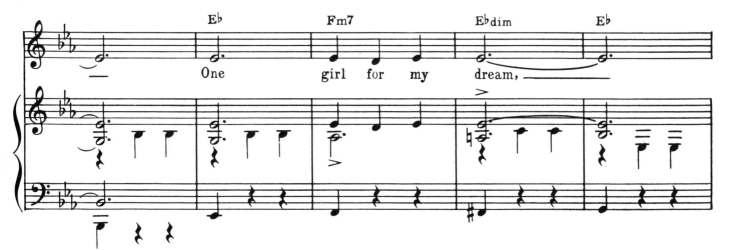

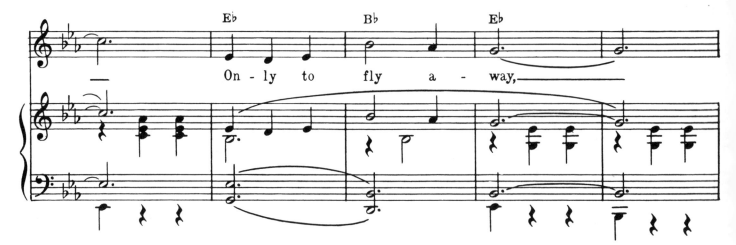

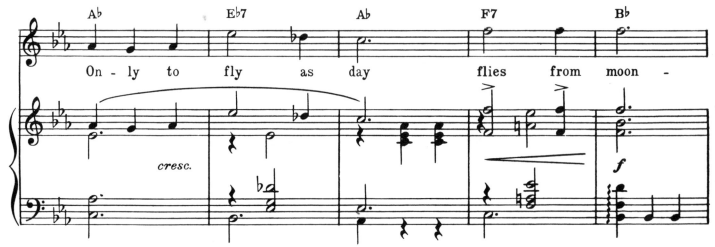

Still say - ing that par - a - dise ____ Once near - ly was

Final Ending *To Verse*

mine. mine. ____ mine. So

Verse

clear and deep are my fan - cies ____ Of things I

wish __ were true. ____ I'll keep re - mem - b'ring

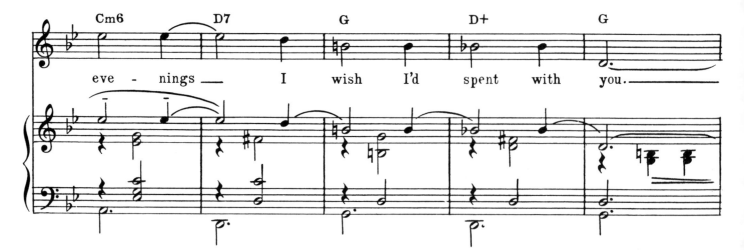

eve - nings ___ I wish I'd spent with you. ___

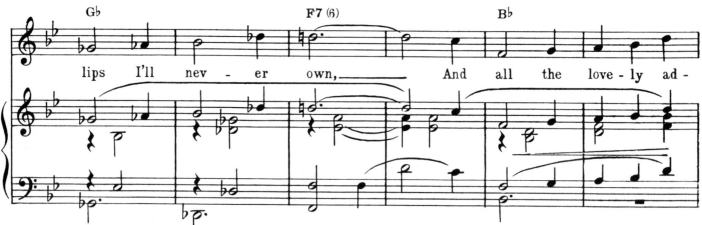

___ I'll keep re - mem - b'ring kiss - es ___ From

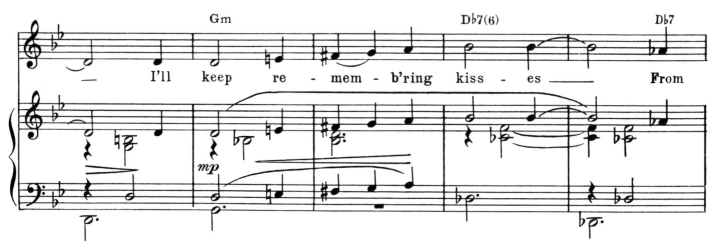

lips I'll nev - er own, ___ And all the love - ly ad -

ven - tures ___ That we have nev - er known. ___

YOU'LL NEVER WALK ALONE
from CAROUSEL

Lyrics by OSCAR HAMMERSTEIN II
Music by RICHARD RODGERS

gold - en sky And the sweet sil - ver

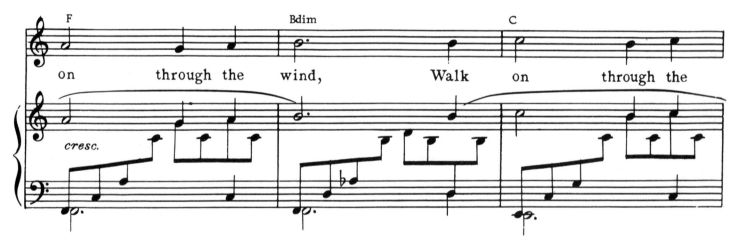

song of a lark. _____ Walk

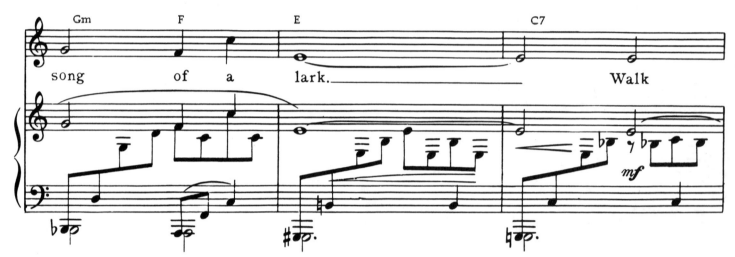

on through the wind, Walk on through the

rain, Tho' your dreams be tossed and

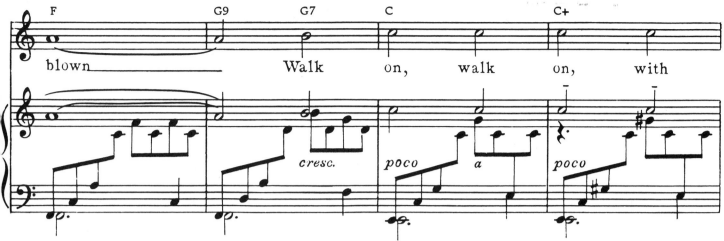

YOU ARE NEVER AWAY

from ALLEGRO

Lyrics by OSCAR HAMMERSTEIN II
Music by RICHARD RODGERS

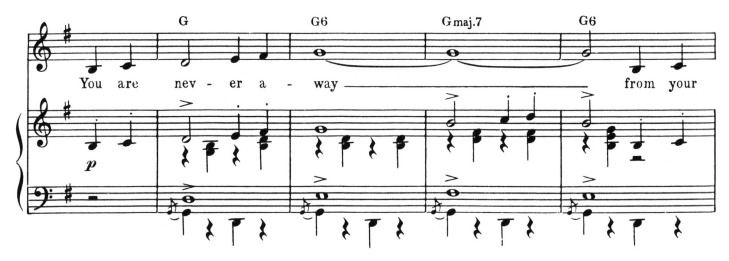

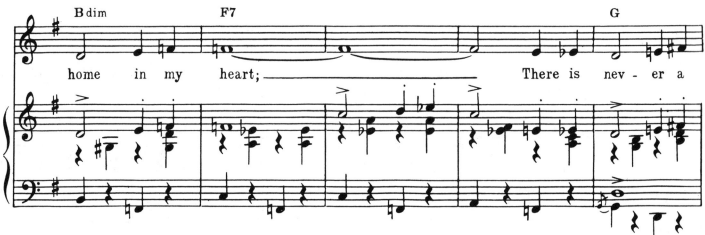

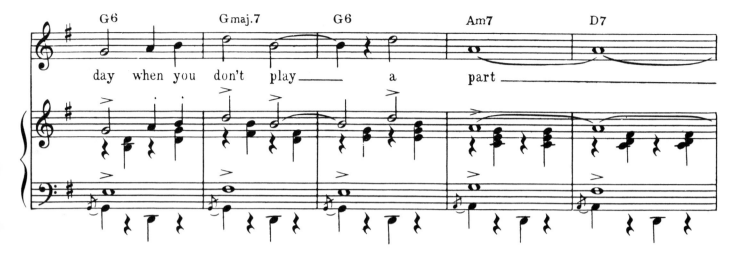

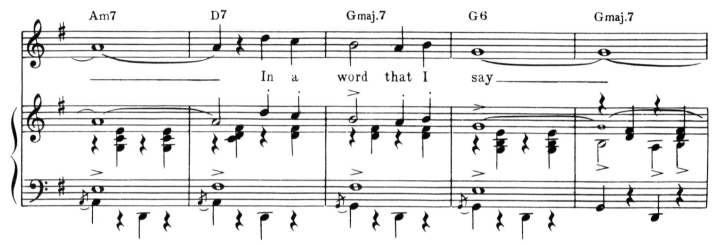

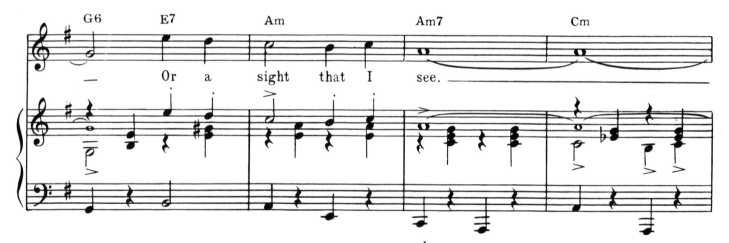

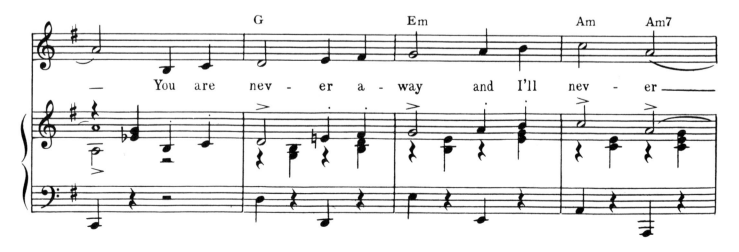

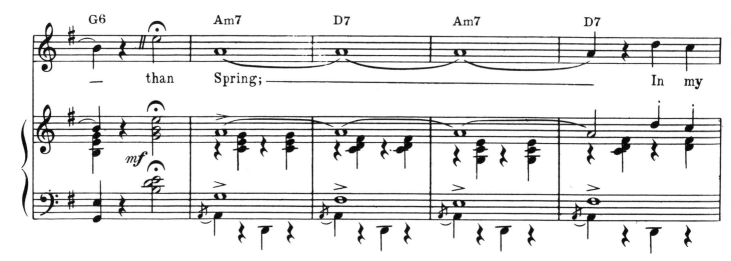

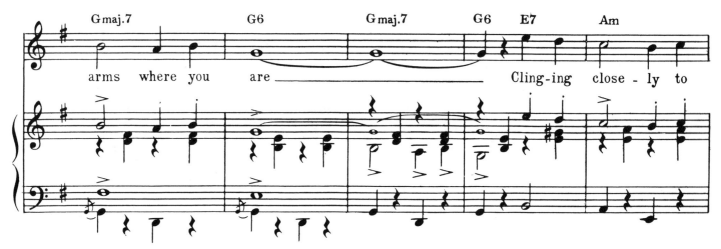

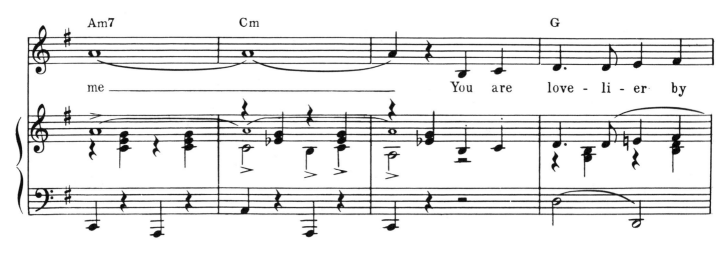

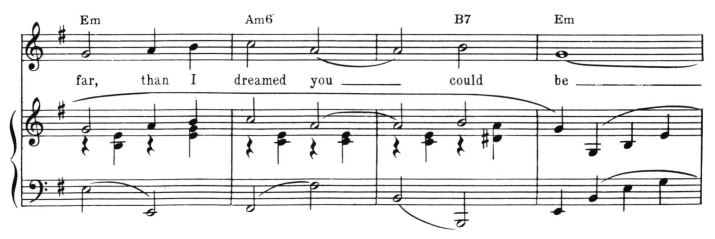

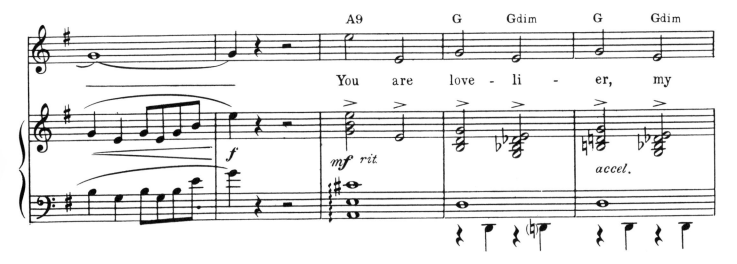

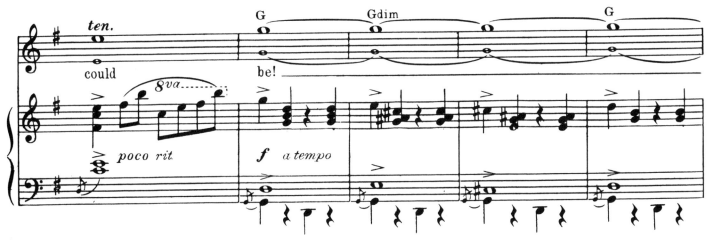

YOUNGER THAN SPRINGTIME

from SOUTH PACIFIC

Lyrics by OSCAR HAMMERSTEIN II
Music by RICHARD RODGERS

I touch your hand And my arms grow strong _____

Like a pair of birds That burst with song. _____

My eyes look down At your love-ly face _____ And I hold the

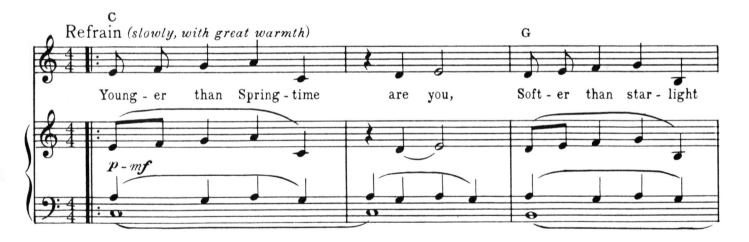

world _____ In my em - brace. _____

Refrain *(slowly, with great warmth)*

Young - er than Spring-time are you, Soft - er than star - light

are you, Warm - er than winds of June are the gen - tle lips you

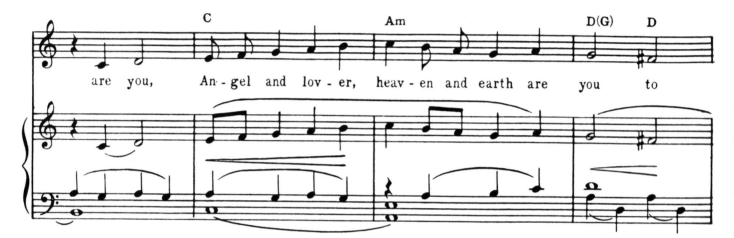

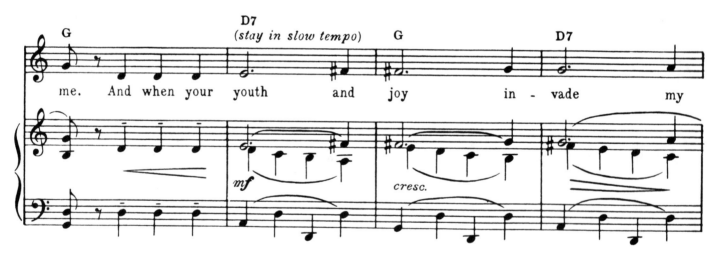

then... Young-er than Spring-time am I, Gay-er than laugh-ter

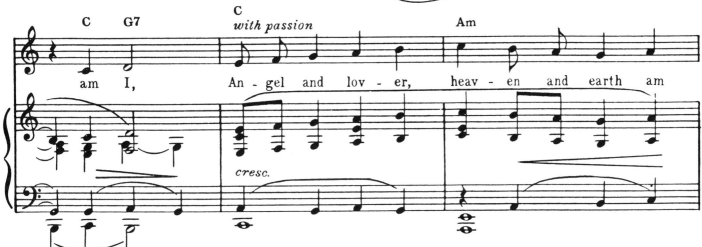

am I, An-gel and lov-er, heav-en and earth am

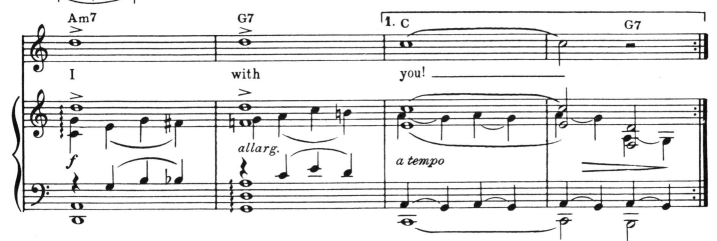

I with you! _____

you! _____